25 First-Grade
PIANO PIECES

Companion Pieces to the "First Solo Book"

BY

Angela Diller
AND
Elizabeth Quaile

ED-1720

ISBN 0-7935-5175-7

G. SCHIRMER, Inc.

DISTRIBUTED BY

HAL•LEONARD®
CORPORATION

7777 W. BLUEMOUND RD. P.O. BOX 13819 MILWAUKEE, WI 53213

THE DILLER-QUAILE SERIES

Grade One

The following books and pieces provide a variety of correlated material for the First Grade, comprising piano solos, duets, technical exercises, and a book for writing and reading.

FIRST SOLO BOOK

A collection of folk-tunes. They are chosen as being the best possible material for developing the young student's *musical taste.* In order to facilitate reading, various devices of printing are used to show phrase lengths, the metrical position of dots, etc. All of these points are described in detail in the preface of the book.

FIRST DUET BOOK

Duets for pupil and teacher are of value in arousing and keeping alive the child's interest because they permit him to take part in making real music long before he would otherwise be able to do so. This book corresponds in grade and choice of material to the *First Solo Book.* It contains charming, melodious arrangements of folk-music and easy classics.

FIRST BOOK OF TECHNICAL EXERCISES

Intended to solve some of the difficulties that appear in elementary pieces, with special reference to the pieces of the *First Solo Book.* Important among these difficulties are the smooth transference of a melodic line from one hand to the other, phrasing, staccato-playing, etc. The book is also useful for independent study.

25 FIRST-GRADE PIANO PIECES

Written with the specific needs of the young beginner in mind. They are especially valuable as additional material for such collections as the *First Solo Book,* which is based largely on folk-songs that in their very nature are limited in compass. These pieces are intended to supplement folk-music and to give a sense of the "romantic" as well as to develop the pianism that the student should be acquiring at an early age. The pieces are easy to read and provide much technical variety.

GREEN DUET BOOK

Written for two children of the same grade to play together. The words are printed above both parts throughout, so that the books may be used as song-books. A child can *sing* the primo part while *playing* the secondo as accompaniment.

BAUER-DILLER-QUAILE COURSE, Book II

This book contains many famous melodies for sight-reading, technical exercises, pedal studies, writing lessons, etc. A feature of the book is the pieces to be taught by rote. The preface contains suggestions to the teacher on how to teach a rote piece, and each of the rote pieces is preceded by preliminary exercises.

LINES AND SPACES

The purpose of this book is to give young students practice both in writing and reading notes in order to facilitate the reading of piano music. The unfolding of the subject is highly original and logical.

SHEET MUSIC by Angela Diller

Gossip Joan	Lazy Man
Augustin	Judges' Dance
Morning Song	Come, Sweet Lass
Reap the Flax	Slumber Song

SHEET MUSIC by Elizabeth Quaile and Frederic Hart

The Drum Major	Playing Soldiers
In a Chinese Village	On Your Toes
	Swing Song

A complete list of Diller-Quaile material for *all grades* is printed on the back cover of this book.

PREFACE

This collection of pieces is a set of twenty-five compositions written with the specific needs of the beginning piano student in mind. The pieces are easy to read and provide much technical variety.

They are especially valuable as additional material for such collections as the First Solo Book, which is based largely on folk-songs and dances. Although folk-tunes give the best foundation for developing the young student's musical taste, they are in their very nature limited in compass and in the pianism that he should be acquiring at an early age; therefore, these "companion pieces" are intended to supplement folk-music and to furnish material that is essentially pianistic.

Angela Diller
Elizabeth Quaile

INDEX

25 First-Grade Piano Pieces

Angela Diller and Elizabeth Quaile

John Plays on the Big Bassoon

The Village Festival

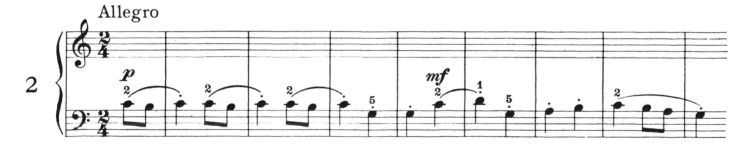

The Playful Kitten

Waltz

Tune and Rhythmic Variations

Andantino
Tune

5

Variation I

Variation II

Variation III (This variation *sounds just like* Variation II. It shows you another way of writing, using dots instead of tied notes. The dot must have exactly the value of the tied note. The tied note is an eighth-note, so the dot must be an "eighth-dot".)

Accompaniment for Tune and Variations

The above study in dotted notes aims to give the student a realization of the "conflict" between the *beats* and the *time-values.*

The Lonely Organ-Grinder

Da Capo al Fine

On a Summer Day

The Roller-Coaster

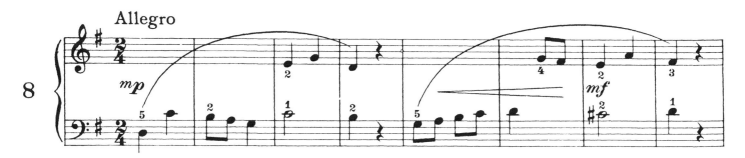

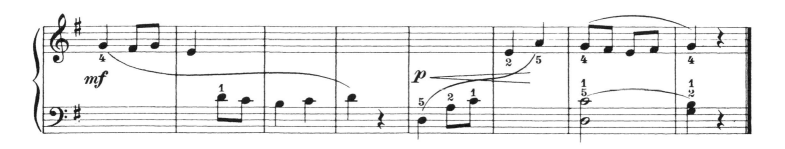

The Puppet-Show

Da Capo al Fine

Tune and Rhythmic Variations

This study aims to give the student the *structural* sense of $\frac{6}{8}$ meter, which, in rapid tempo, has two beats to the measure.

Variation III

Accompaniment for Tune and Variations

The pupil's part must be played an octave higher than written when the accompaniment is used.

The Hunter's Horn

At the Skating Rink

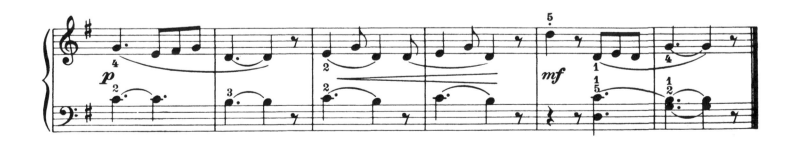

A Country Walk

At Twilight

Gavotte

The Whistling Boy

Scampering

Allegretto

17

Minuet

Andantino

18

Bagatelle

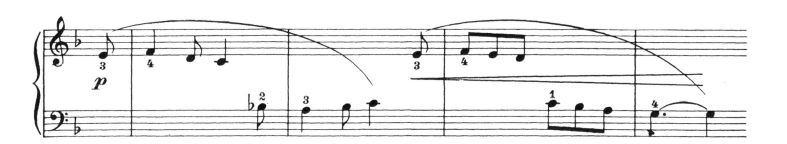

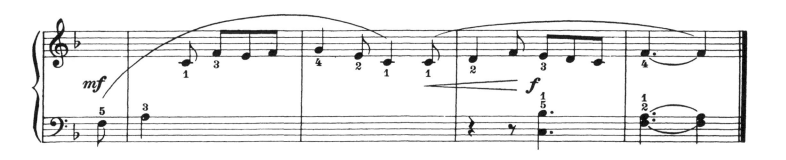

Reverie

20

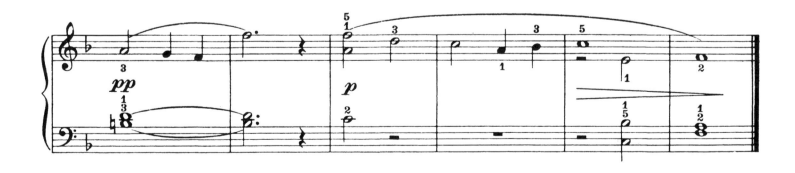

A Morning Walk

Allegretto

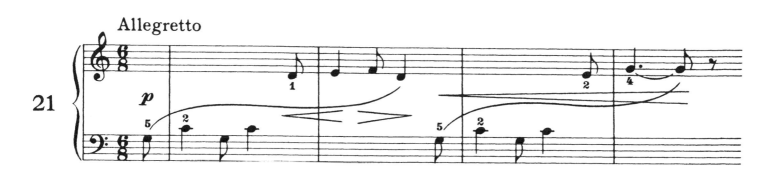

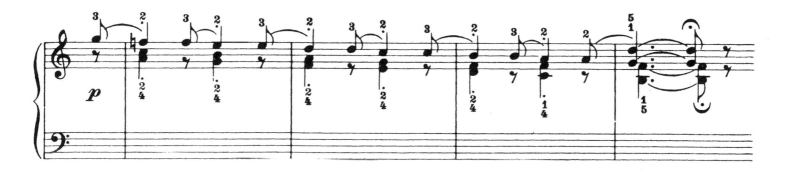

Festival March

The Woodpecker

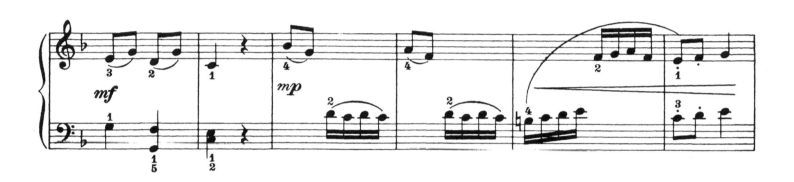

The Land of Nod

Andante con moto

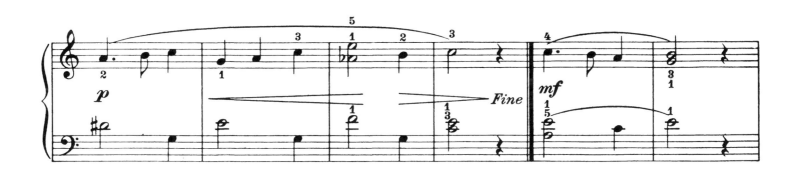

Da Capo al Fine

Irish Reel

D. C. al Fine